To E

On y
birthday

Lots of love
x mum x

Mothers and Daughters

Compiled by Shelley Klein

Michael O'Mara Books Limited

First published in 2005 by
Michael O'Mara Books Limited
9 Lion Yard
Tremadoc Road
London SW4 7NQ

A CIP catalogue record for this book is available from the British Library

ISBN 1-84317-201-1

3 5 7 9 10 8 6 4 2

Designed and typeset by Burville-Riley www.burville-riley.com

Printed and bound in the UK by Bath Press

www.mombooks.com

Contents

For my mother,
who has always been there.
Shelley Klein

Preface

The bond between mothers and daughters has always been a singular one; separate from that between mothers and sons due to the sameness of sex and consequently the sharing of common experience. A mother-daughter relationship, if it is a good one, provides the daughter with a role model to whom she can refer throughout her life, and the mother with a soulmate, someone inextricably part of herself and yet miraculously separate. Naturally there are ups and downs along the way; arguments, fallings-out, disagreements, but at heart a good mother-daughter relationship is bound together by a love so strong and an understanding so deep that nothing can tear it apart.

Personally, I am incredibly fortunate to have enjoyed the most wonderful relationship with my own mother; one that has changed and matured as we have both grown older. As an infant I can recall suffering from terrible nightmares – only to be scooped up and placed in my mother's bed, a warm sanctuary into which no bad dreams ever reached. And, or so it appears to me now, a mother's unparalleled ability to comfort her child only increases with time, for these days, I only have to pick up the phone and hear my mother's voice for life to seem inexplicably better.

Many of the pieces included in this volume come from treasured novels that my mother and I discovered together. More than anyone else, I believe it was through her that I began to love books as much as I do. She encouraged me to pick up titles of all shapes and descriptions, never once saying that something wasn't suitable, or was beyond my abilities. I will always be grateful to her for her undisputed support of my academic pursuits. While mothers can be inspirations, and of course our primary role models, they are also sometimes springboards, propelling us to achievements and accomplishments not yet conceived of in a child's mind – and always wanting a better life for their daughters than they themselves have had. Unquestionably, my mother was such a springboard for me.

The collection also explores the notion of what it is to be a mother. Overwhelmingly, the selflessness of maternity is conveyed – that sacrificing of old self to new role which occurs with barely a ripple of protest, so natural and instinctive does it seem – and the emergence of an all-consuming love which grows only more fierce with time.

Time is, of course, the bringer of great changes and the mother-daughter relationship is one which seems singularly able to adapt itself to the inevitable shift of hierarchies and spirits. As a troublesome teenager, for instance, I can recall with horror traipsing round our local town on a perfectly fine day with my (once-idolized) mother holding her umbrella aloft. 'It's what's called being prepared,' she said as yet another passer-by stared at us. 'It's going to rain, it's only a matter of when.'

Like all mothers, mine had a whole gamut of ways in which to embarrass me, or so it seemed. However, as with so many mother-daughter relationships, even those stormy adolescent years had their fair share of sunshine, for when I was fifteen my mother took me to Paris for a week so that together we could explore a new city – a gesture which began a long love affair for me with that place, its art galleries, architecture and food. She allowed me to study things at my own pace and in my own way, yet was always there in the background if I needed guidance. This silent support has always been a remarkable gift of mothers, but it is especially valuable at that time when daughters are learning to become young women in the world, and need support and independence in equal measure.

All of the above are gifts I hope one day to pass on to my own daughters, so that they too can grow up knowing what it is to be loved by a mother whilst at the same time learning to spread their wings and make their own way in the world. But, if truth be told, even after a daughter's wings are spread a mother's work is not complete. From the labours of birth, through toddlerdom and teenage kicks, to a shared womanhood and that strange time of role reversal, a mother is a mother always, no matter how old her 'babies'. Equally, despite flights of freedom and independent living, a mother's love is forever the most comforting and enduring gift to a daughter, of any age – the storm clouds and intermittent raging rows simply to be weathered through, ultimately strengthening this most precious of bonds.

Which brings me neatly to the approach I used to compile this collection. I aspired to illustrate the incredible, ever-changing nature of the mother-daughter relationship and to show it at its best and most inspirational – thus my inclusion of voices such as that of leading women's suffrage campaigner Elizabeth Cady Stanton, whose rejoicing at the birth of a daughter draws on notions of sisterhood as well as her personal bliss. I also wanted to include as wide a variety of voices as possible, from obscure eighteenth-century poets like Mary Lamb to twenty-first-century celebrities such as Meryl Streep and Cameron Diaz, and even a handful of male voices – in particular those of Thomas Hardy and D. H. Lawrence, both of whom have shown the most extraordinary and beautiful insights into the mother-daughter relationship.

In all, I hope this collection will be as great a pleasure to read as it has been to compile, and that every woman who picks it up will draw inspiration from its pages.

Shelley Klein, 2005

CHAPTER ONE

Giving Birth to

Love

Life began with waking up and loving my mother's face.

George Eliot

Suddenly she was here. And I was no longer pregnant; I was a mother. I never believed in miracles before.

Ellen Greene

The actress Liv Ullmann is best known for her work with the eminent Swedish film director Ingmar Bergman, with whom she had a daughter, Linn Ullmann. The public side of her life is well-documented, but in her autobiography she reveals private memories and reflections, including the wonderful experience of giving birth to her daughter.

How can I explain the enormous feeling of security in knowing that now she was with me in the world? Soon her bed would stand next to mine. We would fall asleep hand in hand. We would listen to music and look at beautiful pictures together. We would discuss everything in life, and find the answers in long confidential conversations. Linn and I would help each other be real people.

Liv Ullmann, Changing – An Autobiography *(1977)*

When I gave birth to my first daughter Frieda, it was as if I had given birth to love. I had never known such strong emotions.

Susan Baxter

Truth, which is important to a scholar, has got to be concrete. And there is nothing more concrete than dealing with babies, burps and bottles, frogs and mud.

Jean J. Kirkpatrick

When I think of my daughter as a baby, I think of all the beautiful things in the world: a clear blue sky, a posy of violets, ducklings, rosebuds, marshmallows and fairy cakes.

Phoebe Moore

When I stopped seeing my mother with the eyes of a child, I saw the woman who helped me give birth to myself.

Nancy Friday, My Mother/My Self (1977)

Having a baby makes you forgive your own mom fast.

Ana Gasteyer

Elizabeth Cady Stanton (1815-1902) is famous for her work with the women's suffrage movement in America, as well as being active in winning property rights for married women and for liberalizing the divorce laws in order that women could leave abusive marriages. In 1840 she married the anti-slavery campaigner Henry B. Stanton and together they produced seven children; five boys and two girls. In these extracts from her letters, it can be seen just how overjoyed she was at the birth not only of her daughter, but later in life that of her granddaughter too.

I am at length the happy mother of a daughter. Rejoice with me all Womankind, for lo! a champion of thy cause is born. I have dedicated her to this work from the beginning. I never felt such sacredness in carrying a child as I have this one, feeling all the time strongly impressed with the belief that I was cherishing the embryo of a mighty female martyr ... She is the largest and most vigorous-looking child I have ever had, weighing 12 lbs with her clothes, and yet my labor was short and easy.

Elizabeth Cady Stanton on the birth of her fifth child, Selected Papers *(1852)*

Thirty years later, upon the birth of her granddaughter in France, she penned the following note to the newborn child:

3 May 1882

My precious baby, You have no idea what a commotion the announcement that 'Elizabeth Cady Stanton' had planted her little foot on French soil created, in our household this morning. 'Vive Elizabeth' rang from garret to cellar. You have no idea my pretty one how we have longed and watched for your arrival ... But you have come at last and we are all so delighted that you belong to the superior sex ... I shall use my influence with your mother to see that you have a free and happy life ...'

Elizabeth Cady Stanton

When you fold your hands,
Baby Louise!
Your hands like a fairy's,
so tiny and fair,
With a pretty, innocent, saint-like air,
Are you trying to think of some
angel-taught prayer
You learned above, Baby Louise?

Margaret Eytinge, 'Baby Louise'

Love twisted suddenly ... inside her,
compelling her to reach into the crib
and lift up the moist, breathing
weight ... The smells of baby powder
and clean skin and warm flannel
mingled with the sharp scent
of wet nappy.

Rosie Thomas

We are not born all at once, but by bits. The body first, and the spirit later... Our mothers are racked with the pains of our physical birth; we ourselves suffer the longer pains of spiritual growth.

Mary Antin

I've never felt anything like it in my life, it's an amazing love. I'm going to slow down. I can't picture going back to work any time soon.

Gwyneth Paltrow *after the birth of her daughter, Apple*

In the sheltered simplicity of the first days after a baby is born, one sees again the magical closed circle, the miraculous sense of two people existing only for each other.

Anne Morrow Lindbergh

I think she has passed the acme of her life – when all is over and the little firstborn darling lies nuzzling and cooing by one's side.

Elizabeth Gaskell in a letter to Charles Norton, whose wife had just given birth, 1863

The moment a child is born, the mother is also born. She never existed before. The woman existed, but the mother, never. A mother is something absolutely new.

Rajneesh

A mother's treasure is her daughter.

Catherine Pulsifer

There is power that comes to women when they give birth. They don't ask for it, it simply invades them. Accumulates like clouds on the horizon and passes through, carrying the child with it.

Sheryl Feldman

Until I gave birth to my daughter, I had always felt like half a person, but when the nurse laid Beth next to me wrapped up like a wet kitten, suddenly I became whole; I was complete.

Rosemary Wiggins

Mother is food; she is love; she is warmth; she is earth. To be loved by her means to be alive, to be rooted, to be at home.

Erich Fromm

A mother understands what a child does not say.

Jewish proverb

D.H. Lawrence (1885-1930) was one of the finest authors of the twentieth century, writing, amongst other literary classics, Sons and Lovers *(1913),* Women in Love *(1920) and* Lady Chatterley's Lover *(expurgated edition 1928). Below, however, is a brief extract from* The Rainbow, *which sums up beautifully the mother-daughter bond and that rapturous moment when a woman becomes a mother for the very first time.*

She did not mind that the baby was not a boy. It was enough that she had milk and could suckle her child; Oh, oh, the bliss of the little life sucking the milk of her body! Oh, oh, oh the bliss, as the infant grew stronger, of the two tiny hands clutching, catching her blindly yet passionately at her breasts, of the tiny mouth seeking her in blind, sure, vital knowledge, of the *sudden consummate peace as the little body sank, the mouth and throat sucking, sucking, sucking, drinking life from her to make a new life, almost sobbing with passionate joy of receiving its own existence, the tiny hands clutching frantically as the nipple was drawn back, not to be gainsaid. This was enough for Anna. She seemed to pass off into a kind of rapture of motherhood, her rapture of mothcrhood was everything.*

D. H. Lawrence, The Rainbow *(1915)*

Anna was my first child and therefore it was she who taught me how to become a mother. We learnt together and she was the most patient of teachers, always smiling and gurgling, despite my complete incompetence at changing nappies or getting her bottles ready on time!

Mary Anne Green

CHAPTER TWO

Toddlers and

Tantrums

When Alicia was going through the terrible twos, I think I loved her even more than before. All that frustrated emotion; her little hands would fist up, her whole body would go rigid and she would scream and stomp her feet. I knew exactly how she felt only I wasn't at liberty to express myself quite so openly!

Rosalind Harper

She was about four months old. Newborns make those breathy, fluttering noises that are so amazing: they're like butterfly wings fluttering. We were in the garden playing with the dogs and, all of a sudden, she let out this raucous laugh. It was like she suddenly found her voice.

Alex Kingston

Mary Wollstonecraft (1759-97) was already a writer of some standing before she gave birth to her first daughter, Fanny, at the age of thirty-five. Fanny's father was an American by the name of Gilbert Imlay, but the relationship was doomed from the start owing to his infidelity. Notwithstanding these unfortunate beginnings, Mary Wollstonecraft determined to bring up her daughter as best she could, guided by principles of a rational nature and by equal amounts of affection. The lessons she wrote for Fanny (extracted below) were a direct product of these objectives. They were published after Mary's death in 1797 following the birth of her second daughter (this time to William Godwin), who later became Mary Shelley, author of Frankenstein.

Lesson VII

When you were hungry, you began to cry, because you could not speak. You were seven months without teeth, always sucking. But after you got one, you began to gnaw a crust of bread. It was not long before another came pop. At ten months you had four pretty white teeth, and you used to bite me. Poor mamma! Still I did not cry, because I am not a child, but you hurt me very much. So I said to papa, it is time the little girl should eat. She is not naughty, yet she hurts me. I have given her a crust of bread, and I must look for some other milk.

The cow has got plenty, and her jumping calf eats grass very well. He has got more teeth than my little girl. Yes, says papa, and he tapped you on the cheek, you are old enough to learn to eat? Come to me, and I will teach you, my little dear, for you must not hurt poor mamma, who has given you her milk, when you could not take anything else.

Lesson X

See how much taller you are than William. In four years you have learned to eat, to walk, to talk. Why do you smile? You can do much more,

*you think: you can wash your hands
and face. Very well. I should never
kiss a dirty face. And you can comb
your head with a pretty comb you
always put by in your drawer. To be
sure, you do all this to be ready to
take a walk with me. You would be
obliged to stay at home, if you could
not comb your own hair. Betty is busy
getting the dinner ready, and only
brushes William's hair, because he
cannot do it for himself.
Betty is making an apple-pye. You
love an apple-pye; but I do not bid
you make one. Your hands are not
strong enough to mix the butter and
flour together; and you must not try
to pare the apples, because you
cannot manage the great knife.
Never touch large knives: they are
very sharp, and you might cut your*

finger to the bone. You are a little girl, and ought to have a little knife. When you are as tall as I am, you shall have a knife as large as mine; and when you are as strong as I am, and have learned to manage it, you will not hurt yourself.

You can trundle a hoop, you say; and jump over a stick. O, I forgot! – and march like the men in the red coats, when papa plays a pretty tune on the fiddle.

Mary Wollstonecraft, The Works of Mary Wollstonecraft

sense of pain
Out of a grieved soul.

Thou straggler into loving arms,
Young climber-up of knees
When I forget thy thousand ways
Then life and all shall cease.

Mary Lamb

[When Connie was maybe two or three] she was this beautifully funky little person who loved to dance and spin and climb all over the couch like it was a mountain ... Connie was the best hugger when she was two. Just the best. She'd wrap her little arms around my neck and squeeze and squeeze and squeeze: 'Hug, Mommy!' I loved that so much.

Chris Bohjalian, Midwives (1997)

You may have tangible wealth untold;
Caskets of jewels and coffers of gold.
Richer than I you can never be
I had a mother who read to me.

Gillian Strickland

To love the tender heart
hath ever fled,
As on its mother's breast the
infant throws
Its sobbing face, and there in sleep
forgets its woe.

Mary Tighe

Simone de Beauvoir (1908-86), a French novelist, essayist and philosopher, was a lifelong campaigner for the rights of women and a hugely influential feminist. In the following passage from her memoirs, a reflective de Beauvoir shares her childhood memories of her mother.

My mother, more distant and more capricious, inspired the tenderest feelings in me; I would sit upon her knees, enclosed by the perfumed softness of her arms, and cover with kisses her fresh youthful skin. Sometimes, beautiful as a picture, she would appear at night beside my bed in her dress of green tulle decorated with a single mauve flower, or in her scintillating dress of black velvet covered with jet. When she was angry with me she gave me a 'black look'; I used to dread that stormy look which disfigured her charming face: I needed her smile.

Simone de Beauvoir, Memoirs of a Dutiful Daughter *(1958)*

As a toddler I loved my father dearly, but my mother was who I looked up to. I think even then I knew instinctively she was the wisest woman on earth.

Jane Walters

CHAPTER THREE

A Pillar of

Strength

If I could bear your pain, I would. If money could buy solutions or my comfort salve the worst hurts, then they would be there for you. It hurts me not to help, and it hurts me to know that all my kindnesses would be inhibiting to your growth. I'll always be there for you. I hope you know, but you are free – you must grow away.

Helen M. Exley

She thought her mother looked wonderfully beautiful with her back to the leafy window. There was something comforting in the sight of her that Linda felt she could never do without. She needed the sweet smell of her flesh, and the soft feel of her cheeks and her arms and shoulders still softer.

Katherine Mansfield, Prelude (1916)

A mother's love for her child is like nothing else in the world. It knows no law, no pity, it dares all things and crushes down remorselessly all that stands in its path.

Agatha Christie

My mother's a teacher and wants her girl to have a secondary education. 'You have to go to high school.' What was enough for her is not enough for her daughter.

Marguerite Duras, The Lover (1984)

Margaret Mitchell (1900-1949) wrote just one book in her lifetime, Gone With The Wind, *which was published in mid-1936 to huge critical and public acclaim. Notwithstanding the fact that the story is set against the backdrop of the American Civil War and therefore deals with the many political issues of that time, what shines through most clearly is the feisty, indomitable spirit of the novel's heroine Scarlett O'Hara, who kicks against her very traditional upbringing while also being formed by it. For Scarlett, no one is more influential than her mother, Ellen – as the following extracts reveal.*

Sometimes when Scarlett tiptoed at night to kiss her tall mother's cheek, she looked up at the mouth with its too short, too tender upper lip, a mouth too easily hurt by the world,

and wondered if it had ever curved in silly girlish giggling or whispered secrets through long nights to intimate girlfriends. But no, that wasn't possible. Mother had always been just as she was, a pillar of strength, a fount of wisdom, the one person who knew the answers to everything.

and from later in the book

'You must be more gentle, dear, more sedate,' Ellen told her daughter. 'You must not interrupt gentlemen when they are speaking, even if you do think you know more about matters than they do. Gentlemen do not like forward girls.'

Margaret Mitchell, Gone With The Wind *(1936)*

Other girls my age were becoming women, flirts, sirens – at least girls – without trouble, and some avidly; it was my mother's cross that I had to be nagged there inch by recalcitrant inch. Daintiness, my mother said, was its essence; once a woman's daintiness got through to a man, all consummations devoutly to be wished for – such as a trousseau of one's own triple-monogrammed tea napkins – soon followed.

Hortense Calisher, 'Songs My Mother Taught Me' (1959)

All you need is love. Love is all you need. A child should be governed by love, as my mother so often said, explaining her methods to us.

Doris Lessing, Under My Skin (1994)

Whenever I am finding life difficult, or I am about to give up I remember my mother. 'Chin up,' she would say, wagging her finger at me and smiling. 'You are my daughter and you will get through this no matter how tough the going gets.'

Patricia Lodge

[A] woman may plant her body [in the kitchen] day after day, but her mind should be sprouting elsewhere. Which is how my mother trained the minds of her daughters.

Nora Seton, The Kitchen Congregation – A Memoir *(2000)*

A mother is not a person to lean on, but a person to make leaning unnecessary.

Dorothy C. Fisher

Everybody knows that a good mother gives her children a feeling of trust and stability. She is their earth. She is the one they can count on for the things that matter most of all. She is their food and their bed and the extra blanket when it grows cold in the night; she is their warmth and their health and their shelter; she is the one they want to be near when they cry. She is the only person in the whole world in a whole lifetime who can be these things to her children. There is no substitute for her. Somehow even her clothes feel different to her children's hands from anybody else's clothes. Only to touch her skirt or her sleeve makes a troubled child feel better.

Katharine Butler Hathaway

All the earth, though it were full of kind hearts, is but a desolation and a desert place to a mother when her only child is absent.

Elizabeth Gaskell

The story of Demeter, the goddess of agriculture, and her daughter Persephone is one of the greatest classical myths of all time.

While wandering in the fields near her home, Persephone is kidnapped by Hades, the god of the dead, and taken to live as his bride in his underworld kingdom. Wild with grief and worry at her daughter's sudden disappearance (as described in the passage below), Demeter relentlessly searches the entire planet for her child, finally coming across the old witch, Hecate, who tells her of her daughter's fate. Demeter and Hades eventually come to an agreement which resolves the tale: Persephone will stay half the year with her mother in the sun and spend the remaining time in Hades' underground kingdom. During this latter period, the earth would remain cold and barren due to Demeter's grief at losing her daughter for a whole six months, yet it would blossom and flourish every time mother and daughter were reunited. According to Greek myth, this is why the seasons are split into the autumn/winter and spring/summer divides.

The heights of the mountains and the depths of the sea ran with [Persephone's] immortal voice: and her queenly mother heard her. Bitter pain seized her heart, and she rent the covering upon her divine hair with her dear hands: her dark cloak she cast down from both her shoulders and sped, like a wild-bird, over the firm land and yielding sea, seeking her child. But no one would tell her the truth, neither god nor mortal man; and of the birds of omen none came with true news for her. Then for nine days queenly Deo wandered over the earth with flaming torches in her hands, so grieved that she never tasted ambrosia and the sweet draught of nektaros, nor sprinkled her body with water. But

*when the tenth enlightening dawn
had come, Hecate, with a torch in her
hands, met her, and spoke to her and
told her news.*

Homeric Hymn to Demeter,
translated by Hugh G. Evelyn-White

*My father explained everything, but
my mother never did, which only
convinced me that she had the
answers but wouldn't tell.*

Margaret Atwood, Surfacing (1979)

The very word 'Motherhood' has an emotional depth and significance few terms have. It bespeaks nourishment and safety and sheltering arms. It embraces not only the human state but the animal kingdom – the tiger fiercely protective of her cubs, the hen clucking over her brood and spreading her wings to shield them from the storm. It speaks of the very beginnings of life in egg or womb and of nurture in the most critical stages thereafter.

Marjorie Holmes

If I had a patch of fabric for every good quality my mother embodies I could make a quilt larger than the whole USA.

Aida Clarke

Mama exhorted her children at every opportunity to 'jump at de sun'. We might not land on the sun, but at least we would get off the ground.

Zora Neale Hurston

My mother, Martha, is the rock on which I have built my life.

Victoria Graham

It's the three pairs of eyes that mothers have to have [...] One pair that see through closed doors. Another in the back of her head ... and, of course, the ones in front that can look at a child when he goofs up and reflect 'I understand and I love you' without so much as uttering a word.

Erma Bombeck

For mother's sake the child was dear,
And dearer was the mother for
the child.

Samuel Taylor Coleridge

Life is the fruit she longs
to hand you,
Ripe on a plate.
And while you live,
Relentlessly she understands you.

Phyllis McGinley

A mother doesn't give a damn about
your looks. She thinks you are
beautiful, anyway.

Marion C. Garretty

My mum is one of the most courageous women I know. She's so strong. She's so emotional and passionate about everything in her life. Sometimes we hate each other and then other times we love each other so much it's ridiculous.

Charlotte Church

Some mothers are kissing mothers and some are scolding mothers, but it is love just the same, and most mothers kiss and scold together.

Pearl S. Buck

*Oh my son's my son till he gets a wife,
But my daughter's my daughter all her life.*

Dinah Mulock Craik

My mother always told me ... 'Aim high! Dare to be different!' She was the rare kind of wonderful mother you can talk to about your sex life, but since I was six or seven, I've felt very protective of her.

Anonymous, from an interview in My Mother/My Self *(1977)*

Mummy herself has told us that she looked upon us more as her friends than her daughters. Now that is all very fine, but still, a friend can't take a mother's place. I need my mother as an example which I can follow. I want to be able to respect her.

Anne Frank, The Diary of a Young Girl *(2002 edition)*

Mother love is the fuel that enables a normal human being to do the impossible.

Marion C. Garretty

Most often it is daughters who turn to their mothers for help and advice, but I have found lately, now that my daughters are grown-up, that they are a wonderful source of help and encouragement. They keep me in touch with all the latest publications, they insist I accompany them on mad shopping sprees and when the phone is out of order or there is a power-cut, they are immediately on the case, phoning up the relevant authorities and giving them a stiff talking-to on my behalf.

Alison Greenwood

We are together, my child and I. Mother and child, yes, but sisters really, against whatever denies us all that we are.

Alice Walker

What do girls do who haven't any mothers to help them through their troubles?

Louisa May Alcott

CHAPTER FOUR

Only One

Mother

When I think of my mother, a million things spring to mind. For instance sapphires because she loves the colour blue; fudge because she has a sweet tooth; pussycats because she loves to have one in her lap; Charles Dickens – all of whose novels she's read; and Mozart and marshmallows which she always enjoys in tandem on cold winter days in front of the fire.

Rachel Jennings

Mamma at the piano. She who was much younger than I realized. With longings I only now perceive when it is too late to share them.
Stories on the edge of the bed. Cocoa and bread and butter with bananas and apple jelly. A woman sitting bowed over a book, her head with short brown hair turned slightly away from me. Looking up now and then and smiling.
That was happiness.

Liv Ullmann, Changing – An Autobiography *(1977)*

My mother wanted me to be her wings, to fly as she never quite had the courage to do. I love her for that. I love that she wanted to give birth to her own wings.

Erica Jong

Angela Carter (1940-1992) was an author whose inimitable style of writing and retelling of fairy stories marked her out as one of the most exceptional novelists of her generation. In the following two extracts (the first recalling her own mother), Carter illustrates just how strongly the mother-daughter relationship mattered to her, not only in real life, but in her fiction as well.

Of all the presents of all the birthdays of a petted childhood, the rose tree is the one I remember best and it is mixed up now with my memory of [my mother], that, in spite of our later discords, our acrimonious squabblings, once she gave me a perennial and never-fading rose tree, the outlines of which, crystallized in the transforming well of memory, glitter as if with properties she herself may not have been at all aware of, a present like part of herself she did not know about that she could still give away to me.

Angela Carter, 'The Mother Lode' (1976)

My eagle-featured, indomitable mother; what other student at the conservatoire could boast that her mother had outfaced a junkful of Chinese pirates, nursed a village through a visitation of the plague, shot a man-eating tiger with her own hand and all before she was as old as I?

Angela Carter, The Bloody Chamber *(1979)*

'That's my mother,' thought Prue. Yes; Minta should look at her; Paul Rayley should look at her. That is the thing itself, she felt, as if there were only one person like that in the world; her mother.

Virginia Woolf, To the Lighthouse *(1927)*

You never realize how much your mother loves you till you explore the attic – and find every letter you ever sent her, every finger painting, clay pot, bead necklace, Easter chicken, cardboard Santa Claus, paperlace Mother's Day card and school report since day one.

Pam Brown

At the height of her powers Elizabeth Barrett Browning (1806-61) far outshone her husband Robert Browning as a poet in the public's estimation. Sadly, however, like so many women writers of this and earlier generations (for example, Jane Austen and Charlotte Brontë, to name but two), she never had any children and died while still relatively young. Her childlessness was no barrier to creative empathy though, and here in perhaps her most famous poem, Aurora Leigh, she paints the most charming portrait of what it is to be a mother.

Women know
The way to rear up children
(to be just);
They know a simple, merry,
tender knack
Of tying sashes, fitting baby-shoes,
And stringing pretty words that
make no sense,
And kissing full sense into
empty words;
Which things are corals to cut
life upon,
Although such trifles.

Elizabeth Barrett Browning, Aurora Leigh (1857)

When they were first published, Laura Ingalls Wilder's (1867-1957) nine Little House *books were an instant success and have remained a firm favourite with children and adults to this day. Semi-autobiographical in content, the stories centre on the tight-knit Ingalls family: Ma, Pa and their three little girls, Mary, Laura and Carrie. Pa is the traditional breadwinner and protector, but Ma is revealed by her daughter to be equally strong; caring for her daughters, cooking, cleaning, keeping house, and beyond everything else letting them know how much they are loved.*

It was so queer to be put to bed in the daytime, and Laura was so hot that everything seemed wavering. She held on to Ma's neck while Ma was undressing her, and she begged Ma to tell her what was wrong with her. 'You will be all right. Don't worry,' Ma said, cheerfully. Laura crawled into bed and Ma tucked her in. It felt good to be in bed. Ma smoothed her forehead with her cool, soft hand and said, 'There, now. Go to sleep.'

Laura Ingalls Wilder, Little House on the Prairie (1935)

My mother used to say, 'He who angers you, conquers you!' But my mother was a saint.

Elizabeth Kenny

[W]ithout a word, they began to push against the ground with their feet, so that the swing began to rock ever so gently. Nothing rambunctious, just a smooth swaying, as if the swing were a cradle holding both mother and daughter, two separate and equal planets tumbling through space on a night in late autumn.

Rebecca Wells, Divine Secrets of the Ya-Ya Sisterhood *(1996)*

A mother is a person who seeing there are only four pieces of pie for five people, promptly announces she never did care for pie.

Tenneva Jordan

Hundreds of stars in the pretty sky,
Hundreds of shells on the
shore together,
Hundreds of birds that go singing by,
Hundreds of birds in the
sunny weather.

Hundreds of dewdrops to greet
the dawn,
Hundreds of bees in the purple clover,
Hundreds of butterflies on the lawn,
But only one mother the wide
world over.

Anonymous, 'Only One Mother'

Of all the female authors in the French language, Sidonie Gabrielle Colette (1873–1954) is perhaps the best known, the most loved. Over the years she wrote a number of highly successful novels including Claudine at School *(1900),* Cheri *(1920) and* Gigi *(1945), but many people consider, quite rightly in my opinion, that her memoirs* My Mother's House *and* Sido *are the most accomplished and compelling works, centring as they do on the loving, powerful figure of her mother, who was not only extremely influential on the rural community in which she lived, but also on her daughter.*

'Beauty' my mother would call me, and 'Jewel-of-pure-gold'; then she would let me go, watch her creation – her masterpiece, as she said – grow smaller as I ran down the slope.

Colette, My Mother's House *(1922)*

*They do say that children like you,
who have been carried so high in the
womb and have taken so long to come
down into the daylight, are always
the children that are most loved,
because they have lain so near their
mother's heart and have been so
unwilling to leave her.*

Colette, Sido (1930)

*A mother's love! What can compare
with it! Of all things on earth, it
comes nearest to divine love
in heaven.
A mother's love means a life's
devotion – and sometimes a life's
sacrifice – with but one thought, one
hope and one feeling, that her
children will grow up healthy and
strong, free from evil habits and able*

to provide for themselves. Her sole
wish is that they may do their part
like men and women, avoid dangers
and pitfalls, and when dark hours
come, trust in Providence to give
them strength, patience and courage
to bear up bravely.

Happy is the mother when her heart's
wish is answered, and happy are sons
and daughters when they can feel that
they have contributed to her noble
purpose, and in some measure, repaid
her unceasing, unwavering love
and devotion.

Anonymous

CHAPTER FIVE

Victorian and

Edwardian

Mothers and

Daughters

Virginia Woolf (1882-1941) was one of the foremost authors ever to have graced the pages of English literature. As with other great novelists, she had the gift of imagining herself in roles far removed from that of her own – and never is this more clearly illustrated than in her novel To the Lighthouse, *where she depicts the motherly Mrs Ramsay constantly reflecting on the lives of her daughters and sons (Virginia Woolf, though married, never had children). Here, Mrs Ramsay is considering her youngest daughter, Rose.*

But she let them take their time to choose: she let Rose, particularly, take up this and then that, and hold her jewels against the black dress, for this little ceremony of choosing jewels, which was gone through every night, was what Rose liked best ... She had some hidden meaning of her own for attaching great importance to this choosing what her mother was to wear. What was the reason, Mrs Ramsay wondered, standing still to let her clasp the necklace she had chosen, divining, through her own past, some deep, some buried, some quite speechless feeling that one had for one's mother at Rose's age.

Virginia Woolf, To the Lighthouse *(1927)*

A mother is one to whom you hurry when you are troubled.

Emily Dickinson

Kate Douglas Wiggin (1856-1923) was not only a prolific children's author, but also organized the first free nursery schools on the Pacific coast circa 1878 and was a teacher of some renown herself. She will always be best remembered for her novel, Rebecca of Sunnybrook Farm, *from which the following extract is taken. Here, Rebecca's mother, Aurelia, reflects on who her daughter is, finding it difficult to identify this glorious girl as her own offspring.*

Aurelia could have understood the feeling of a narrow-minded and conventional hen who has brought a strange, intrepid duckling into the world; but her situation was still more wonderful, for she could only compare her sensations to those of some quiet, brown Dorking who has brooded an ordinary egg and hatched a bird of paradise. Such an idea had crossed her mind more than once during the past fortnight, and it flashed to and fro this mellow October morning when Rebecca came into the room with her arms full of golden-red and flaming autumn leaves.

Kate Douglas Wiggin, Rebecca of Sunnybrook Farm (1903)

None but mothers know each other's feelings when we give up our daughters whom we love and cherish so tenderly to the mercies of a man, and perhaps even a stranger.

Emmeline B. Wells

Elizabeth von Arnim (1866-1941) was one of the best-loved writers of her day. Here, in an extract taken from her most successful novel, is just one of the delightful portraits she painted of her children.

The babies each had a kitten in one hand and an elegant bouquet of pine needles and grass in the other, and what with the due presentation of the bouquets and the struggles of the kittens, the hugging and kissing was much interfered with. Kittens, bouquets, and babies were all somehow squeezed into the sleigh, and off we went with jingling bells and shrieks of delight.

'Directly you comes home the fun begins,' said the May baby, sitting very close to me. 'How the snow purrs!' cried the April baby, as the horses scrunched it up with their feet. The June baby sat loudly singing 'The King of Love my Shepherd is', and swinging her kitten round by its tail to emphasise the rhythm.

Elizabeth von Arnim,
Elizabeth and Her German Garden *(1898)*

A few days after the engagement was announced Mrs Honeychurch made Lucy and her Fiasco come to a little garden-party in the neighbourhood, for naturally she wanted to show people that her daughter was marrying a presentable man.

E. M. Forster, A Room with a View *(1908)*

Few children's writers have achieved the success and popularity of Edith Nesbit (1858-1924) whose works number among them The Treasure Seekers *(1899),* The Phoenix and the Carpet *(1904) and most famously* The Railway Children *(1906). In the latter, Nesbit portrays a close-knit family unit and sensitively explores the enduring, never-forgotten nature of the mother-daughter relationship.*

Mother did not spend all her time in paying dull calls to dull ladies, and sitting dully at home waiting for dull ladies to pay calls to her. She was almost always there, ready to play with the children, and read to them, and help them to do their home-lessons. Besides this she used to write stories for them while they were at school, and read them aloud after tea, and she always made up funny pieces of poetry for their birthdays and for other great occasions, such as the christening of the new kittens, or the refurnishing of the doll's house, or the time when they were getting over the mumps.

and a little later in the story

'Are you fonder of us than Granny was of you when you were little?' Phyllis asked. Bobbie made signs to her to stop, but Phyllis never did see signs, no matter how plain they might be. Mother did not answer for a minute.

*She got up to put more water
in the teapot.
'No one,' she said at last, 'ever loved
any one more than my mother
loved me.'
Then she was quiet again, and Bobbie
kicked Phyllis hard under the table,
because Bobbie understood a little bit
the thoughts that were making Mother
so quiet – the thoughts of the time
when Mother was a little girl and was
all the world to her mother. It seems so
easy and natural to run to Mother
when one is in trouble. Bobbie
understood a little how people do not
leave off running to their mothers when
they are in trouble even when they are
grown up, and she thought she knew a
little what it must be to be sad, and
have no mother to run to any more.*

E. Nesbit, The Railway Children *(1906)*

Did the sun always shine?
I can't remember
A single cloud that dimmed the
happy blue –
A single lightening-bolt or
peal of thunder,
To daunt our bright, unfearing lives:
can you?

We quarrelled often, but made
peace as quickly,
Shed many tears, but laughed the
while they fell,
Had our small woes, our childish
bumps and bruises,
But Mother always 'kissed and
made them well.'

Susan Coolidge, What Katy Did (1872)

CHAPTER SIX

Like Mother,

Like Daughter

Thou art thy mother's glass,
and she in thee
Calls back the lovely April
of her prime.
William Shakespeare

The woman who bore me is no longer
alive, but I seem to be her daughter in
increasingly profound ways.
Johnnetta Betsch Cole

In search of my mother's garden I
found my own.
Alice Walker

Jane Austen (1775-1817) never knew the joys of motherhood herself, however this did not prevent her from creating some of the most memorable mother-daughter relationships in literary history, in particular the loving bond between Elinor and Marianne Dashwood with Mrs Dashwood in Sense and Sensibility *(below) and, as seen later in this collection, that of the Bennet girls with Mrs Bennet in* Pride and Prejudice.

Elinor, this eldest daughter ... possessed a strength of understanding, and coolness of judgment, which qualified her, though only nineteen, to be the counsellor of her mother, and enabled her frequently to counteract, to the advantage of them all, that eagerness of mind in Mrs Dashwood which must generally have led to imprudence. She had an excellent heart; her disposition was affectionate, and her feelings were strong; but she knew how to govern them: it was a knowledge which her mother had yet to learn; and which one of her sisters had resolved never to be taught.

Marianne's abilities were, in many respects, quite equal to Elinor's. She was sensible and clever; but eager in everything: her sorrows, her joys, could have no moderation. She was generous, amiable, interesting: she was everything but prudent. The resemblance between her and her mother was strikingly great.

Jane Austen, Sense and Sensibility *(1811)*

I cannot sing, my mother could not sing, and her mother before her.

Margaret Drabble

The older I get, the more of my mother I see in myself. The more opposite my life and my thinking grow from hers, the more of her I hear in my voice, see in my facial expression, feel in the emotional reactions I have come to recognize as my own.

Nancy Friday, My Mother/My Self (1977)

There is a point where you aren't as much mom and daughter as you are adults and friends.

Jamie Lee Curtis

Ellen Bawtry, born Ellen Cudworth, was happy with this, for Ellen liked her children to be quiet and good. She did not like Bessie to play on the street with the rough ones. She claimed that the street was dirty ... Ellen, like her daughter Bessie, disliked dirt.

Margaret Drabble, The Peppered Moth *(2000)*

Part of us resents forever the fact that we and our mothers were closer than we can ever be to any other creature. They gave us freedom – but we sense the hidden bond, and know it's unbreakable.

Pam Brown

A daughter is a mother's gender partner, her closest ally in the family confederacy, an extension of herself. And mothers are their daughters' role model, their biological and emotional road map, the arbiter of all their relationships.

Victoria Secunda

There still faintly beamed from the woman's features something of the freshness, and even the prettiness, of her youth; rendering it probable that the personal charms which Tess could boast of were in main part her mother's gift, and therefore unknightly, unhistorical.

'I'll rock the cradle for 'ee, mother,' said the daughter gently. 'Or I'll take off my best frock and help you wring

up? I thought you had finished long ago.'

Her mother bore Tess no ill-will for leaving the housework to her single-handed efforts for so long; indeed, Joan seldom upbraided her thereon at any time, feeling but slightly the lack of Tess's assistance whilst her instinctive plan for relieving herself of her labours lay in postponing them. Tonight, however, she was even in a blither mood than usual. There was a dreaminess, a pre-occupation, an exaltation, in the maternal look which the girl could not understand.

Thomas Hardy, Tess of the D'Urbervilles *(1891)*

I would love to grow up to be like my mother and why not, for she is everything I admire in a woman; intelligent, kind, beautiful and funny. If I grow up to reflect even an eighth of what she represents, I will be happy.

Karen Armstrong

CHAPTER SEVEN

Humorous

Observations

I think it is rather difficult for a short mother to have a very tall daughter. They are always bending down their swan-like necks to you or putting things on shelves you can't reach and taking such long strides you can't keep up with them. I think it is almost impossible not to develop an inferiority complex and to become a bit of a tyrant by way of compensation. You can neither effectively cuddle or scold a creature a head taller than yourself who seems to be almost out of earshot. I feel like a hen who's hatched a crane.

Antonia White, Diaries I *(1948)*

And in this place it may be as well to apprise the reader, that Miss Fanny Squeers was in her three-and-twentieth year. If there be any one grace or loveliness inseparable from that particular period of life, Miss Squeers may be presumed to have been possessed of it, as there is no reason to suppose that she was a solitary exception to a universal rule. She was not tall like her mother, but short like her father; from the former she inherited a voice of harsh quality, and from the latter a remarkable expression of the right eye, something akin to having none at all.

Charles Dickens, Nicholas Nickleby *(1838)*

Motherhood is the strangest thing; it can be like being one's own Trojan horse.

Rebecca West

Don't tell your kids you had an easy birth or they won't respect you. For years I used to wake up my daughter and say, 'Melissa, you ripped me to shreds. Now go back to sleep.'

Joan Rivers

[Fanny Price] might scruple to make use of the words, but she must and did feel that her mother was a partial, ill-judging parent, a dawdle, a slattern, who neither taught nor restrained her children, whose house was the scene of mismanagement and discomfort, [who had] no talent, no conversation, no affection toward [Fanny] herself.

Jane Austen, Mansfield Park *(1814)*

At the tender age of eighteen, Françoise Sagan (1935-2004) hit the French literary scene with the novella Bonjour Tristesse. *It was an immediate success, being translated into twenty languages and selling over 2 million copies. Slightly arch in style, it sums up beautifully the angst of a teenage girl, but here, in an extract from an interview with Sagan, the writer recalls her own childhood and in particular her mother, with a far greater tenderness than is shown in her fictional works.*

Then there were the air raids. Usually, we didn't bother going down to the cellar as my mother claimed it was a waste of time. But one day the bombing was so heavy that she said, 'Perhaps we should, after all, for the children's sake.' She'd just set her hair, I remember. So we went down to the cellar. The walls were shaking and bits of plaster were falling everywhere. Everyone was in tears. But my mother was quite calm and we played cards. We really enjoyed it. We weren't at all frightened. When we went back up to the apartment,

there was a mouse in the kitchen.
My mother fainted; she's terrified
of mice.

Françoise Sagan, Réponses – An Autobiography *(1974)*

Grown don't mean nothing to a
mother. A child is a child. They get
bigger, older, but grown. In my heart
it don't mean a thing.

Toni Morrison

How the mother is to be pitied who
hath handsome daughters! Locks,
bolts, bars, and lectures of morality
are nothing to them: they break
through them all. They have as much
pleasure in cheating a father and
mother, as in cheating at cards.

John Gay

The television series Absolutely Fabulous, *created by comedienne Jennifer Saunders, brought to the viewing public the most wonderfully awful mother-daughter relationship; one in which the roles were reversed to the extent that the long-suffering daughter Saffy had to take on the parental role, while her mother Edina stomped about like a spoilt teenager.*

Edina Monsoon: *Sweetie, make mama a cup'a'coffee. You're so clever and you know where everything is, don't you? I think it's marvellous that you know where things are.*
I think you're marvellous.
Saffron Monsoon: *Flattery won't turn me into your slave. The coffee is on the table in front of you. Pick up a spoon, put coffee in cup, pour on boiling water...*
Edina Monsoon: *...and scald my hand and get third degree burns, screaming in agony. Do you really want THAT on your conscience this morning, darling?*

from Absolutely Fabulous *(1992)*

'Do ladies,' she asks her mother carefully, 'still do it even when they don't want to have any more babies?' 'Well' – there was a swelling pause – 'well, some do and some don't.'

Carol Shields, The Stone Diaries *(1993)*

When a woman has five grown up daughters, she ought to give over thinking of her own beauty.

Jane Austen, Pride and Prejudice *(1813)*

That dear octopus from whose tentacles we never quite escape, nor in our innermost hearts ever quite wish to.

Dodie Smith

Happy for all her maternal feelings was the day on which Mrs Bennet got rid of her two most deserving daughters. With what delighted pride she afterwards visited Mrs Bingley and talked of Mrs Darcy may be guessed. I wish I could say for the sake of her family, that the accomplishment of her earnest desire in the establishment of so many of her children, produced so happy an effect as to make her a sensible, amiable, well-informed woman for the rest of her life; though perhaps it was lucky for her husband, who might not have relished domestic felicity in so unusual a form, that she still was occasionally nervous and invariably silly.

Jane Austen, Pride and Prejudice *(1813)*

Neurotics build castles in the air, psychotics live in them. My mother cleans them.

Rita Rudner

CHAPTER EIGHT

Famous Mothers

and Daughters

To describe my mother would be to write about a hurricane in its perfect power.

Maya Angelou

I've learned so much from my mother. She's got a clear, rooted perspective on life and showbusiness and I think I inherited my point of view from her.

Gwyneth Paltrow on her mother Blythe Danner

Motherhood has a very humanizing effect. Everything gets reduced to essentials.

Meryl Streep

It really bothers me when I see people doing my mother in drag. I mean, just imagine if you saw people doing that with your mother.

Chastity Bono

It was no great tragedy being Judy Garland's daughter. I had tremendously interesting childhood years – except they had little to do with being a child.

Liza Minnelli

I stopped believing in Santa Claus when at age six my mother took me to a department store to see him and he asked me for my autograph.

Shirley Temple

My first job is to be a good mother.

Faye Dunaway

I fly her out to LA for the premieres, because she and dad just love that. And they were all in New York to see a Christmas Spectacular with the Rockettes. You know, I think my mom is a frustrated Rockette! I'm very close to her.

Catherine Zeta Jones

And so our mothers and grandmothers have, more often than not anonymously, handed on the creative spark, the seed of the flower they themselves never hoped to see – or like a sealed letter they could not plainly read.

Alice Walker

My mom is the nicest person on the face of the earth. She treats everybody the same.

Cameron Diaz on her mother, Billie

Once I got past my anger toward my mother, I began to excel in volleyball and modelling.

Gabrielle Reece

To me luxury is to be at home with my daughter, and the occasional massage doesn't hurt.

Olivia Newton-John

She's so strong and really instilled in me a sense of strength. And she continues to do that. And she taught me to persevere, to never quit. I may be down for a little bit, but I'll always rise again thanks to her.

Halle Berry on her mother, Judith

When a child enters the world through you, it alters everything on a psychic, psychological and purely practical level.

Jane Fonda

I think she's so smart, her instincts are so good. I think wherever they lead her, that's the right place to be.

Blythe Danner on her daughter Gwyneth Paltrow

I was stunned when I saw on the ultrasound a tiny, living creature spinning around in my womb. Tap-dancing, I think. Waving its tiny arms around and trying to suck its thumb. I could have sworn I heard it laughing.

Madonna on seeing her daughter Lourdes on the ultrasound

I believe my mother is still involved in my life. I lost her when I was twenty-three. It was a huge loss for me because we had become very close. I am convinced that all the great things that happened in my life have come to me through her angelic intercession.

Andie MacDowell

She's like this perfection, this utter purity that's uncorrupted by anything.

Courtney Love speaking about her daughter Frances Bean

She's my teacher, adviser, and greatest inspiration.

Whitney Houston speaking about her own mother

She's my mom, I'm her daughter, and we're damned proud of each other.

Kate Hudson on her relationship with her mother, Goldie Hawn

CHAPTER NINE

Motherly Advice

and Advice to all

Mothers

Never grow a wishbone, daughter,
where your backbone ought to be.
Clementine Paddleford

If you have never been hated by your
child, you have never been a parent.
Bette Davis

Mothers, look after your daughters,
keep them near you, keep their
confidence — that they may be true
and faithful.
Elmina S. Taylor

Daughters can sometimes be too
serious: teach them to laugh and not
take life too seriously.
Catherine Pulsifer

Don't put your daughter on the stage, Mrs Worthington.

Noel Coward

The only advice I would give my mother is not to die, because then she would have to watch her daughter coping alone, and without my mother's advice I know everything I did would turn out disastrously!

Ethel Benning

The story of a mother's life: trapped between a scream and a hug.

Cathy Guisewite

Hope has two beautiful daughters.
Their names are anger and courage;
anger at the way things are, and
courage to see that they do not
remain the way they are.

Saint Augustine

A mother who is really a mother
is never free.

Honoré De Balzac

If my daughter, Liza, wants to become
an actress, I'll do everything
to help her.

Judy Garland

Mother is the name for God in the lips and hearts of little children.

William Makepeace Thackeray

When your mother asks, 'Do you want a piece of advice?' it is a mere formality. It doesn't matter if you answer yes or no. You're going to get it anyway.

Erma Bombeck

CHAPTER TEN

The Dying of the Light

Hester Thrale (1741-1821) is probably most famous for her friendship with Dr Samuel Johnson, who treasured their relationship and took a great interest in Hester's twelve children. Hester herself, while a devoted mother, was perhaps more firmly attached to her own mother, although, as the extract below reveals, as her daughters grew older she became ever more aware of the support and consolation they selflessly offered. This piece is extracted from Her Family Book – *a diary which Johnson encouraged Hester to keep every day.*

My mother's Illness has lately increased so fast that it has required all my Attention and shall have it – My Children I shall keep, My Mother is leaving me, and Filial Duty shall not be cheated of its due, what Gratitude do I not owe her? what Esteem have I not of Her? what Tenderness do I not feel for her? Oh my sweet Mother! I have now past many days and Nights in her room in her Room [sic], while Mr Thrale proceeded with his Affairs in London – they thank God do mend every day, but nobody can guess what a Winter this has been to me, and big with Child too again God help me! This morning therefore finding myself incapable of attending to every body, and every thing, I fairly resolved to walk up the Common with Harry to Dr Thomas who keeps a Boy's School here; and may get more: he will likewise go on with his Writing more commodiously there, while I give to my Mother my undivided attention; and She seems vastly delighted too that She has lived to see him a School-boy. As for Hetty, She already knows so much of History, Geography, Astronomy and Natural Philosophy; that she begins now to study for her own sake, and does not so much require keeping to Hours as younger Children do; She has besides a sort of every-day-Wit; a degree of Prudence, Discretion and common Sense, that I have seldom seen in a Girl even of twelve or thirteen Years old[1], which makes her a most comfortable Child; in spite of her bad Temper and cold heart; I really can consult her and often do – She is so very rational.

Hester Thrale, 21 March 1773

I knelt before her, kissed her dear hand and placed it next to my cheek. But though she opened her eyes she did not, I think, know me.

Queen Victoria, with reference to the death of her mother, March 1861

1 Hetty Thrale was nine years old at the time

It doesn't matter how old I get, whenever I see anything new or splendid, I want to call, 'Mom, come and look.'

Helen M. Exley

Recently I persuaded my mother to purchase a walking stick. For too long she has put off this moment, but now gripping it firmly in her right hand she takes enormous pleasure in beating the earwigs out of my dahlias, no matter that the blooms fly off as well.

Eleanor Baxter

I miss thee, my Mother!
Thy image is still
The deepest impressed on my heart.
                    Eliza Cook

The children had not any Mamma.
She had died when Phil was a baby,
four years before my story began.
Katy could remember her pretty well;
to the rest she was but a sad, sweet
name, spoken on Sunday, and at
prayer-times, or when Papa was
specially gentle and solemn.

Susan Coolidge, What Katy Did *(1872)*

That lovely voice; how I should weep
for joy if I could hear it now!
                    Colette

That a woman of ninety-six was lucky enough to die an easy death without losing her wits or the ability to enjoy her chosen way of life in her own house: there was nothing much to mourn in that. Naturally I miss my mother – would often catch myself thinking that I must tell her something amusing or ask her something important – but I would also come to feel that mothers are never quite lost.

Diana Athill, Yesterday Morning (2002)

A mother's love for the child of her body differs essentially from all other affections, and burns with so steady a flame that it appears like the one unchangeable thing in this earthly mutable life, so that when she is no longer present it is still a light to our steps and a consolation.

W. H. Hudson

Most of all the beautiful things in life come by twos and threes, by dozens and hundreds. Plenty of roses, stars, sunsets, rainbows, brothers and sisters, aunts and cousins, comrades and friends – but only one mother in the whole world.

Kate Douglas Wiggin

Bibliography

ALCOTT, LOUISA MAY
   Little Women (Oxford World's Classics, 1998)
ARNIM, ELIZABETH VON
   Elizabeth and Her German Garden (Virago Modern Classics, 1996)
ATHILL, DIANA
   Yesterday Morning (Granta Books, 2000)
ATWOOD, MARGARET
   Surfacing (Virago Press, 1979)
AUSTEN, JANE
   Mansfield Park (Norton Critical Editions, 1998)
   Pride and Prejudice (Penguin Popular Classics, 1994)
   Sense and Sensibility (Penguin Popular Classics, 2004)

BEAUVOIR, SIMONE DE
   Memoirs of a Dutiful Daughter, translated by James Kirkup
   (André Deutsch and Weidenfeld and Nicolson, 1959)
BOHJALIAN, CHRIS
   Midwives (Vintage, 1998)
BOWEN, ELIZABETH
   Pictures and Conversations, copyright © 1974 by Spencer
   Curtis Brown and Curtis Brown Limited, Executors of the
   Estate of the late Elizabeth Bowen (Allen Lane, 1975)
BROWNING, ELIZABETH BARRETT
   Aurora Leigh (Academy Chicago Publications, 1987)

CALISHER, HORTENSE
   'Songs My Mother Taught Me', from *The Collected Stories
   of Hortense Calisher* (Donadio and Ashworth, Inc., 1959)

CARTER, ANGELA
  The Bloody Chamber (Vintage, 1995)
  'The Mother Lode', *New Review* (1976)
COLETTE, SIDONIE GABRIELLE
  My Mother's House, translated by Una Vicenzo Troubridge and
  Enid McLeod (Farrar, Straus and Giroux, 1953)
  Sido, translated by Una Vicenzo Troubridge and Enid McLeod
  (Farrar, Straus and Giroux, 1953)
COOLIDGE, SUSAN
  What Katy Did (Wordsworth Editions Limited, 1994)

DICKENS, CHARLES
  Nicholas Nickleby (Penguin Popular Classics, 1994)
DRABBLE, MARGARET
  The Peppered Moth (Viking, 2000)
DURAS, MARGUERITE
  The Lover, translation by Barbara Bray (Fontana Paperbacks, 1986)

FORSTER, E. M.
  A Room With A View (Penguin Modern Classics, 1998)
FRANK, ANNE
  The Diary of a Young Girl, translated by Susan Massotty
  (Puffin, 2002)
FRIDAY, NANCY
  My Mother/My Self (Delacorte Press, 1977)

HARDY, THOMAS
  Tess of the D'Urbervilles (Oxford World's Classics, 1994)
'HOMERIC HYMN TO DEMETER'
  translated by Hugh G. Evelyn-White (Loeb Classical Library, 1914)

LAWRENCE, D. H.
  The Rainbow (Penguin Books Limited, 1976)

LESSING, DORIS
Under My Skin: Volume One of My Autobiography, To 1949
(HarperCollins Publishers, 1994)

MANSFIELD, KATHERINE
'Prelude', from *The Short Stories of Katherine Mansfield*
(The Ecco Press, 1983)
MITCHELL, MARGARET
Gone With The Wind (Pan Books Limited, 1974)

NESBIT, E.
The Railway Children (Puffin Classics, 1994)

SAGAN, FRANÇOISE
Réponses – The Autobiography of Françoise Sagan,
translated by David Lacey (The Ram Publishing Company,
Black Sheep Books, 1979)
SETON, NORA
The Kitchen Congregation – A Memoir (Weidenfeld and
Nicolson, 2000)
SHIELDS, CAROL
The Stone Diaries (Fourth Estate, 1993)
STANTON, ELIZABETH CADY
*The Selected Papers of Elizabeth Cady Stanton and
Susan B. Anthony* (Rutgers University Press, 2000)
SAUNDERS, JENNIFER
Absolutely Fabulous (BBC Books, 1993)

THRALE, HESTER
Diary extracts featured in *Parents and Children,*
edited by Claire Tomalin (Oxford University Press, 1981)

ULLMANN, LIV
  Changing – An Autobiography, translated by the author in
  collaboration with Gerry Bothmer and Erik Friis
  (Weidenfeld and Nicolson, 1977)

WELLS, REBECCA
  Divine Secrets of the Ya-Ya Sisterhood (Pan Books, 2000)
WHITE, ANTONIA
  Diaries 1926-1957, Volume One, edited by Susan Chitty
  (Constable, 1991)
WIGGIN, KATE DOUGLAS
  Rebecca of Sunnybrook Farm (Wordsworth Editions Limited, 1994)
WILDER, LAURA INGALLS
  The Little House On The Prairie (HarperCollins Publishers, 1963)
WOLLSTONECRAFT, MARY
  The Works Of Mary Wollstonecraft (New York University Press, 1989)
WOOLF, VIRGINIA
  To the Lighthouse (Penguin Books Limited, 1996)

I am also indebted to the following websites:

http://www.houseofquotes.com

http://www.mothers.net

http://www.quotationlibrary.com

http://www.worldofquotes.com